GARDEN PORTRAITS
EXPERIENCES OF NATURAL BEAUTY

GARDEN PORTRAITS
EXPERIENCES OF NATURAL BEAUTY

LARRY LEDERMAN

FOREWORD BY GREGORY LONG
TEXT BY THOMAS CHRISTOPHER

THE MONACELLI PRESS

Opening spreads:

Pages 2-3: Rock Cobble Farm.

Pages 4-5: Merrin Garden, entrance.

Pages 6-7: Hawks Nest.

Pages 8-9: Wisteria arbor and labyrinth, Sleepy Cat Farm

Page 10: Maple collection, Iroki.

First published in the United States by The Monacelli Press. All rights reserved.

Library of Congress Control Number: 20209377552
ISBN: 9781580935456

Design: Susan Evans, Design per se

Printed in China

The Monacelli Press
65 Bleecker Street
New York, New York 10012

TONE POEMS

GREGORY LONG

Commitment to their designed places out of doors, sometimes over one lifetime, sometimes over several generations: this is the dedication of the makers, owners, and stewards of the gardens in this book. And in this book, we also see a complementary commitment by the photographer to the task of capturing the essence of these places. Larry Lederman has conceived this project and created these photographs to explore these twin commitments, one of them his own.

This is Lederman's sixth book of photographs. After a long and distinguished career as a corporate lawyer, he decided ten years ago to pursue a gentler path. His first two projects are books we created together—they are beautiful and lasting views of the gardens, trees, and landscapes of the New York Botanical Garden, and they are the authoritative visual records of that historic place as it looked between 2000 and 2015.

The evocative photographs in this book are documentary to be sure, but in these images, Lederman has also focused on the design and art of the sixteen gardens he wants us to see. It is essential to understand that he was not assigned to photograph any of these places. On the contrary, he found them himself—gardens that have been created, tended, and developed over long periods of time by their devoted stewards.

What these places all have in common is that they are large, luxuriant, and complex. They are all varied in elements—water, woodland, meadow, farm field, the long view, flower gardens, specimen trees,

orchards, fine hardscape. Richly layered and satisfyingly biodiverse, these gardens and landscapes are perfect subjects for photographic tone poems.

In considering these photographic essays, it is interesting to analyze Lederman's method, to quantify his commitment of time and creative energy, and to appreciate his taste. After selecting the gardens, he sets out to learn and understand them. He visits in all seasons, in all weather, at many times of day, in many light conditions. He wants to analyze their design and study their character. He wants to know their plants and see their environmental conditions and visual elements from many points of view. He wanders. He walks the paths, forward and backward, and stops frequently so that his camera can memorize views and details. At the New York Botanical Garden during the years that he worked on our books, we would watch this process, and we grew to love his devotion to the place. As a result of this time spent and such intense scrutiny, he sometimes discovers aspects of a place that the residents themselves have never seen or fully appreciated. In his lyrical photographs of NYBG over the years, garden horticulturists and I were sometimes not sure the pictures he presented were actually shot in our garden. "Is this our crabapple collection?" "How did he find this view we have never seen?" "Where is this sweetgum tree?" We were often amazed and delighted. I think the owners of the gardens in this book will see vistas, patterns, designs on the land they did not know they possess. They will love their gardens even more, and their commitments will grow.

Lederman's particular artistic vision is a function of his devotion and method but also, of course, an expression of his taste. He loves paths and walks and steps that lead his eye and yours into the scene. He adores trees and woodland gardens, reflections in water, slightly disorganized mass plantings of flowers. He can't wait every year to revisit these places on lush days in the autumn, when water and woodland views are at their richest. He likes the expression of movement in small spaces and the diagonal presentation of straight edges canted up across the image. In a very special and original way, he also sees and emphasizes pattern and abstraction in nature. Winter views and woody plants shot up close illustrate his gift for transforming the familiar into the unrecognizable. Some of these images remind me of the American landscapes of Neil Welliver. They are painterly.

Lederman often sees and shows us foreground, middle ground, and distant spaces in the same frame. "This is how I see it," the photograph says to us. In a less documentary mode, he also sometimes flattens out distances between trees and objects with his long lens so that elements that are not close to one another appear to be. He manipulates his view of the scene to create a pattern on the picture plane that is abstract in a sense, intentionally not realistic. Study the various images of Innisfree and find the one black willow which appears again and again, a kind of fulcrum as he moves around the site and as the seasons change. In some shots of the Beckoning Path, there are reflections—collages of water, sky, shiny leaves—that are difficult to recognize or understand. And then there is the wild,

naturalized underplanting of forget-me-not, that bane of many a gardener's existence, presented as a spotted and abstract background to other plantings at Rocky Hills.

This is a special set of garden and landscape photographs. Beautiful and evocative, yes; inspirational to all of us whose gardens at home are still not perfect (will that ever happen?); romantic in the extreme. They are also about an artist's commitment to his own particular method, his own exploration of place, his own vision and taste, his fascination with design out of doors, and his appreciation of nature. The garden portraits here are also very clearly offered up as visual tone poems inspired by places he has come to love.

Native waterlilies abound in a pond next to the garden's central causeway.

WOODLAND GARDEN

HUDSON VALLEY, NEW YORK

Many gardens evolve as they develop. Few, however, change course as dramatically as did this one. Located just an hour and a half north of midtown Manhattan, this garden began as a collection of evergreen trees and a conventional formal landscape around the owner's residence. About the time of his retirement from his business career in the mid 1990s, however, he experienced an epiphany. He had been, in his younger days, an enthusiastic hiker who explored many of the natural wonders of the Appalachian trail, and he had even recreated a southern bald cypress (*Taxodium distichum*) swamp at the (appropriately) southern end of his estate.

When retired, he decided to redesign the core of the property in a naturalistic manner, using native North American plants combined in something like their natural associations or "plant communities" to suggest what he had experienced on the Appalachian trail. To do this, he planted numerous trees and shrubs. The natural streams on the site were amplified, becoming creeks, waterfalls, and ponds.

The plant communities were installed along a north–south axis, suggesting their positions along the Appalachian trail. So, for example, the bald cypress swamp anchors the garden's southern end. Just to the north is the "Azalea Riot," a mimicking of Carolinas landscapes planted with dozens and dozens of different types of native deciduous azaleas (*Rhododendron* spp.), intermingled with specimens of Carolina hemlock (*Tsuga caroliniana*) and native evergreen rhododendrons (*Rhododendron* spp.).

To the north of that lies "Smoke Tree Pond," which is surrounded by American smoke trees (*Cotinus obovatus*) of the south-central Appalachians. These bear puffs of pink-gray flowers in summer before their foliage turns a brilliant scarlet in fall. Like the setting of a jewel, this planting is surrounded by a mix of eastern red cedars (*Juniperus virginiana*), dogwoods (*Cornus florida*), sourwoods (*Oxydendron arboreu*m), bigleaf magnolia (*Magnolia macrophylla*), southern rhododendrons (*R. catawbiense* and *R. carolinianum*), huckleberries (*Gaylussacia* spp.) and a mix of pitch, Virginia, and table mountain pines (*Pinus rigida*, *P. virginiana*, and *P. pungens*).

The family residence lies on what the gardeners refer to as the geographic "Mason-Dixon line," the area where a more northerly vegetation begins. From here northward is a flora of fir trees (*Abies* spp.), eastern hemlock (*Tsuga canadensis*), and red, white, and black spruce (*Picea rubens*, *P. glauca*, and *P. mariana*). This shades into a more boreal forest of firs (*Abies* spp.), maples (*Acer* spp.), larch (*Larix laricina*) with an understory of viburnums (*Viburnum* spp.).

When the redesign of this garden began, the use of native plants was relatively uncommon. The demand that this extraordinary garden created, one former head gardener believes, helped to spur interest among nursery growers, and so helped to promote the wider use of natives by gardeners in general. The creator of this garden may be gone, but his surviving family maintains his botanical garden, thus memorializing this lover of eastern North American plants and scenery.

A spring woodland carpeted with celandine poppies.

Left: A high point overlooking native dogwoods and the Hudson Valley below.

Above: Rugged boulders lend structure to a pond marking the garden's "Mason-Dixon Line," the geographic border between northern and southern plant communities.

Above: The bald cypress swamp in fall as these deciduous conifers drop their needles.

Right: In late spring and summer the water in the bald cypress swamp is covered with waterlily blossoms.

Left: Rock formations dwarf a guest cottage, creating a sense of woodland isolation.

Right: Waterfalls lace the walls of an old quarry.

Above: The "Azalea Riot," filled with color in spring, transplants a Carolina scene to this northern setting.

Right: Native rosebay rhododendrons envelop a pondside bridge.

Left: Mossy steppingstones cross a stream and lead into the heart of a lush grove.

Above: A massive outcrop towers above a native rhododendron, enhancing the bold mountainous impression of the garden.

A causeway through the northern section of the woodland provides a viewing area for autumn's brilliant colors.

A rail fence and a barn reflect the agricultural heritage of Rock Cobble Farm.

ROCK COBBLE FARM

SOUTH KENT, CONNECTICUT

Anne Bass has pieced together her house at Rock Cobble Farm from a historic barn rescued from Pennsylvania, a pair of agricultural buildings that existed on the property, and a one-room schoolhouse. Appropriately, this composite surrounds a cobbled courtyard and overlooks to the west an orchard of fruit trees: apples moved to the site as mature specimens, plus heirloom apples, pears, plums, peaches and cherries purchased as saplings that are still growing in. Around the rest of the house are inscribed a series of garden rooms designed by the eminent modernist landscape architect Dan Kiley and completed after his death by Madison Cox.

Geometrical and formal in style, these rooms are walled and organized by an imaginative collection of hedges: boxwood, of course, but also germander (*Teucrium*), hornbeam (*Carpinus betulus*), and panicle hydrangea (*Hydrangea tardiva*), as well as the larger rectilinear masses of pleached London plane trees (*Platanus x acerifolia* 'Bloodgood'). A rose garden hosts six beds of vintage and modern roses as well as a compromise especially favored by Anne Bass, the David Austin roses which have the beautiful forms and fragrances of old-fashioned roses but also the reblooming habit of the modern types.

The medicinal herb garden is enclosed by espaliered pear trees and centers on a stone basin, a cider press from Normandy that in summertime is filled with water and lotuses. Around the pool are compact parterres with herbaceous plants and boxwood spheres, each one centering on a standard, a tree-like Chinese lilac 'Summer Charm.' Beyond lies a double row of square beds that support the garden's herbs.

A terrace outside the living room of the house, planted with lavenders, serves as a gallery on which to display containers in season. Especially impressive is the cut flower and fruiting shrub garden, with its grape-clad pergola entered through arches of climbing blackberries and clematis and bordered by rugosa roses. Espaliered

33

apples frame beds planted with a seasonal succession of flowers: tulips, irises, peonies, lilies, and dahlias, with accompanying plantings of black, white, and red currants, gooseberries, and red, gold, and black raspberries.

From this formal center the landscape transitions to a more relaxed look harmonious with the agricultural setting. Across a stone-banked stream that supports a collection of alpine plants is a notable collection of some sixty-five different magnolia species and cultivars and a winter walk of paperbark maple (*Acer griseum*) and seven-son flower (*Heptacodium miconioides*), a late summer/fall flowering Chinese shrub with remarkable exfoliating bark. Further along is an informal woodland garden.

The farm's herd of Randall cattle, an heirloom American breed that Anne Bass helped to save from extinction, graze right up to the edge of the gardens, posing a bucolic counterpoint to the strict formality of the plant displays. Stone walls have been reconstructed, and invasive plants rooted out in the surrounding fabric of woods and fields. Special attention has been given to tree planting, with additions along the roadways and across the farm of sugar maples (*Acer saccharum*), yellowwoods (*Cladrastis kentukea*), sweetgums (*Liquidambar styraciflua*), black tupelo (*Nyssa sylvatica*), bald cypress (*Taxodium* spp.) and others.

Throughout, the planting has been designed to restore and preserve the heritage of the setting. What was achieved in this landscape, according to the late owner, was something really important to her: of appropriateness. That is, Anne Bass did not want visitors to walk into the garden and feel as though they had gone to another part of the world. She found planting only natives in her garden too limiting, she said, but even if a plant was not indigenous, it should be similar enough in form, flower, and foliage, to look as if it could have been.

A herd of heirloom Randall cattle grazes a meadow at the garden's edge.

In the orchard, fruit trees serve as
living trellises for climbing roses.
Meticulous pruning has turned this
apple tree into a living sculpture.

Left: Boxwood and germander hedges organize the medicinal herb garden; an old French cider press provides the basin for an aquatic garden.

Right: Along an edge pear trees are espaliered on an elegant wrought-iron frame.

Left: Modern and heirloom roses make the rose garden glorious in June.

Above: A stone trough filled with tropical waterlilies punctuates a path in the cut flower and fruiting shrub garden.

Above: Liquid Amber trees.

Right: An arched gap in a hornbeam hedge opens into the cut-flower and fruiting-shrub garden.

Left: Crossing a stone-banked stream, this path leads from the formal gardens around the house to the more informally arranged plant collections and woodland gardens.

Above: A venerable maple, ablaze with fall foliage, shelters the terrace beside the house.

Along this trail around the lake, breaks in the vegetation provide carefully calculated views.

THE BECKONING PATH

ARMONK, NEW YORK

The creator of this garden, Ted Nierenberg, was explicit in the importance he attached to an artistry of living plants, stones, soil, and water. He wrote that this landscape, twelve acres around a lake in northern Westchester County, was "imagined as a three-dimensional painting." An apt metaphor, for from the ephemeral flowers of spring to the blazing foliages of fall, this is a truly artistic—though ever-changing—composition. Indeed, the house is as much a piece of sculpture as a residence. Designed by Jens Quistgaard, chief designer of Dansk International Designs (Ted Nierenberg was, with his wife, Martha, founder of the famous housewares company), it is a powerful presence nestled among tall trees, emerging from the greenery to anchor many of the garden's views and set the tone.

Whatever Nierenberg's design philosophy, he was determined to get things just right. An avid collector of Japanese maples and rhododendrons, he arranged these plants in the hundreds along the necklace of narrow trails he hacked out by hand with a mattock. Editing was an essential element of the process, as Nierenberg decided that he had placed a tree not quite correctly, whereupon he would dig out its roots and move it to another spot. Even when a tree was properly sited, Nierenberg might spend decades methodically pruning it to better reveal and enhance its structure.

All of this took time. Nierenberg spent more than fifty years perfecting this landscape, which he called *Cobamong*, an Algonquin word meaning "beautiful hidden valley." His planting was lavish, but the effects subtle, achieved through careful balancing, and often the use of the lake's reflective surface to confuse the division between land and sky.

Every season has its special moments of beauty here, although autumn, when the maple leaves color and fall, setting ablaze the ground as well as branches, is perhaps the most spectacular. In a series of vignettes strung together along the paths, Nierenberg employed a sort of ambulatory choreography. The paths dip down to the lake to expose a

view, climb back up to share a vista, then interject a sharp turn where visitors are desired to slow down and look at some detail at their feet.

This is not the first time that this remarkable garden has been photographed. Ted Nierenberg created a portfolio of images that he published as a book, *The Beckoning Path: Lessons of a Lifelong Garden*, in 1993. He characterized these images as "meditations" on what he had learned in Cobamong. They express the mystery and romance of the garden.

One point that Nierenberg's book does make is that this is indeed a lifelong garden. Through his patient and passionate involvement with this site, the land came to echo his tastes and preferences. Gardening, however, is a collaboration and the site leaves its mark upon the maker as well. There is a stubborn persistence in this rocky soil, and a quicksilver quality in the body of water at its heart.

Although Ted Nierenberg died in 2009, his garden, the vast three-dimensional canvas of his half century of efforts, has been preserved by the current owner Jonathan Miller, who has rededicated the property as a private wellness retreat. For a lifelong garden to live on after the death of its creator is a rare achievement, as any student of this art will testify.

Above: Jens Quistgaard's sculptural house sits above mounded rhododenrons and azaleas.

Right: Nierenberg crowned this peninsula with an artificial island just large enough to support a Japanese maple positioned to catch the sunlight and cast a reflection.

Left: Mirrored in the lake's surface, the colors of the maples would confuse the eye, if not for the reference point of the emerging rock.

Right: Shrubs selected for their autumn foliage colors are doubled by the reflection across the lake.

Left: Reflections of clouds whiten the surface of the lake, as glimpsed through this Japanese maple.

Above: Filtered sunlight gilds the lake edge, separating view from reflection.

The delicate harmony of the planting softens a view of the house.

Left: A contemporary "tone poem"; in this moody image, the specimen maple on the island pulls the eye into the frame.

Above: White rhododendron blossoms echo the white of the waterlilies; the reflection of the rhododendron flowers completes the composition.

Recalling the Japanese symbol of the sun, this gate sets the tone of the garden and its surrounding planting.

BRUBECK GARDEN

WILTON, CONNECTICUT

Dave and Iola Brubeck brought their architect, Beverley David Thorne, and a West Coast sensibility with them from California when they moved to Wilton, Connecticut, in 1961. The couple were second-generation native Californians and reluctant to relocate, but as Dave Brubeck's career as a jazz musician and composer took off, he was increasingly busy on the East Coast, and a Connecticut base would allow him to spend more time with his family. Still, their background is visible in the Japanese-inflected design of the house, and in the planting of the five-acre garden around it, which features Japanese classics such as azaleas, a weeping cherry, Japanese maples, a kousa dogwood, and, most memorably, a magnificent katsura tree (*Cercidiphyllum japonicum*) down by the expansive pond the Brubecks dug.

Water, in fact, was what defined this landscape. The site was divided by a pair of natural streams, which came together in a low, moist orchard of decrepit apple trees. The first summer after the house was completed in 1963, Iola Brubeck's father, a California forest ranger, came east to uproot the apples and excavate the pond where they had stood. At the same time the channels of the streams were adjusted, and the one to the west was redirected from its swampy meandering course into a shaded pool, and below that a stepped series of cascades down which it pours before spilling into the pond.

This was how things were done in the making of this retreat: improvisationally, as was appropriate for the home of a jazz musician. And, just like in jazz, repeated motifs create a sense of unity. Tracing the edges of all the waterways are clumps of tall Japanese irises. Likewise, four identical wooden bridges—arched and painted crimson red—span the streams and provide access to an island in the pond. They not only link the grounds together literally, but also create a strong visual rhythm.

This residence was Brubeck's "Shangri-La" according to his son Chris, the family spot to which he retreated from days and nights spent in concerts, clubs, and recording studios. With hardly a window facing

the road, the house looks inward and to the south with a wall of glass affording a view to and embracing the garden. Even Shangri-La, however, could be boisterous. Although the house included a music space with two pianos for composing and a private recording studio, there were also six children, all playing their own instruments. Brubeck retreated again, to the little island in the pond, where he built a compact, one-room cabin where he could compose in peace. This "woodshed" lends a contemplative air to the garden, emphasizing its peaceful and private nature. It also serves as a focal point for views.

For the most part, it was Iola Brubeck who took charge of the planting, working with a local gardener, Emilio Cavicchia, and the personnel at a nearby nursery. The plant list was simple, emphasizing shrubs and trees arranged around the lawn and along mossy, rocky paths. There are a couple of notable specimens: a dawn redwood (*Metasequoia glyptostroboides*) to the west of the house, which in this moist setting has grown to exceptional size, and the katsura by the pond. Keeping the planting simple was a wise decision, for the real interest of this landscape is in the constant movement and sound of the water, a wonderful theme on which to improvise.

Above: Fall lends new colors and a new look to the garden gate.

Left: Flagstone pavers lead toward the entrance gate.

Above: Two streams were channeled
and refined to create the water
effects in the garden.

Right: The back of the house is a
glass wall, uniting building and
garden.

Brubeck did much of his composing in this lakeside cabin.

Dappled, early spring sunlight illuminates the carefully crafted stream and the pond that occupies the site of the former orchard.

Left: The warmer light of mid-spring gives a different aspect to stream and pond.

Above: A view of the house across the pond.

Left: The Japanese gate is set between massive stone piers.

Right: The second stream flows to the pond through a lush, summer-time landscape.

Early spring in the Cullman garden.

CULLMAN GARDEN

DARIEN, CONNECTICUT

When Lewis Cullman died at age one hundred in June 2019, he left a horticultural legacy that reverberates far beyond the house and the nearly five-acre landscape he entrusted to his grandchildren. Among Cullman's many philanthropic causes was a role as vice chairman of the New York Botanical Garden's board, where his donations supported molecular studies of plants and other pursuits. When the Museum of Modern Art was undergoing renovation, it was Lewis Cullman, a member of that institution's board as well, who persuaded the museum to temporarily move the works from its sculpture garden to exhibition at NYBG, an early use of the space for sculptural exhibits.

Cullman's own garden is lighthearted, an indulgence in floral colors. As Joe Haberny, Cullman's gardener for thirty-one years recalls, the garden was a somewhat overgrown field of wildflowers when he first came on board. Under Cullman's direction, he methodically moved through the landscape, creating ordered beds of perennials, including delphiniums, irises, lupines, rudbeckias, and yarrows. Even the best assortment of perennials has its downtimes, though, after one flush of bloom has ended and the next has yet to begin. To ensure constant bloom, Cullman had Haberny interplant with hosts of annuals.

There were ranks of tulips in the spring, then as the season warmed, snapdragons, dragon lady begonias, Mexican heather, blue salvias, angelonias, nicotiana, hollyhocks and sweet potato vines, mandevillas, verbenas and cleomes, as well as more routine flowers such as marigolds, ageratums, impatiens, and petunias. In many cases the plants were purchased in the spring and then held and grown-on to drop into a garden bed later in the summer when a spot of mature color was needed.

Planned to create views from the house, the garden is dotted with sculptures and other focal points, including an architectural detail from a German church. A circumferential path takes visitors around

the garden, under a line of eight meticulously pruned apple trees, and down to a disused quarry at the garden's foot. This became an important feature: filled with water and converted into a swimming pond, the rock basin provides an oasis and a cool visual contrast to the hot floral color.

Perhaps the best assessment of this garden was that of the famed English horticulturist Penelope Hobhouse. To resolve a discussion between Cullman and his wife, Dorothy, about what the garden was lacking, Hobhouse was invited over for an inspection. After strolling about the grounds, she delivered her verdict: "Change nothing."

Above: Entrance to the garden from the cobbled driveway.

Right: The quarry pool is both a swimming pond and a reflecting pool.

Above: Beds of tulips surround an architectural detail salvaged from a German church; as the weather warms, the tulips are replaced by red geraniums.

Right: A sign from an English pub and a whimsical chair and table add notes of humor to this utilitarian potting shed.

Above: Begonias and impatiens
furnish color in a shady spot.

Right: Annuals such as these white
spider flowers and marigolds ensure
that there is color in the garden
throughout the summer.

A perimeter path offers a glimpse of an egret fishing in the pond bordering the Glimcher garden.

GLIMCHER GARDEN

LONG ISLAND, NEW YORK

A multitalented man, Arne Glimcher has successfully pursued two remarkable careers. He is best known, perhaps, as the founder of New York's Pace Gallery, which has under his leadership represented a stellar roster of many of the most important contemporary artists and expanded to multiple locations worldwide. But he is also acclaimed in the film world as a producer of the Academy Award–nominated *Gorillas in the Mist* and as director of *The Mambo Kings.*

Glimcher's theatrical skills and artistic enthusiasms have combined in the five-acre garden that he, with the help and input of his wife, Millie, has created on a site overlooking a Long Island pond. For sourcing plant material he had the assistance of Charlie Marder of Marders, a Bridgehampton nursery and landscape design firm. From the first, Glimcher's intention was in part to create a sculpture garden to display pieces from his collection that were too large to be installed indoors. This evolved as the garden did, with the gardener finding a place for sculptures as he acquired them. Currently, with some dozen in all, the plein air gallery includes works by Alexander Calder, Louise Nevelson, Joan Miró, Julian Schnabel, Henry Moore, Kiki Smith, and Zhang Huan. A small "house" by Jean Dubuffet hearkens back to the centuries-old tradition of garden follies. Presiding over all is the residence, designed by Ulrich Franzen.

It is above all a shade garden, says the creator, and though it does bloom strongly at various times in the summer, it is primarily an essay in texture, scale, and tones of green. Thus, collections of ferns and hostas play an important role, as does a selection of hydrangeas, which bloom throughout the hotter months. "It's like a jungle of images," Glimcher observes, "from lilies to dahlias." And it continues to develop, with the recent addition of a spiral-form flower garden.

Arne Glimcher is on record as saying that "a life in art" was his motivation for founding an art gallery. "I wanted to live with artists," he has said. "I wanted to make beautiful shows." Certainly, in the garden with which he has surrounded his home, he has achieved both.

81

A Louise Nevelson sculpture is installed in a woodland area. *Fallen Warrior* by Henry Moore is sited to be seen from the house and from the pool.

A small structure by Jean Dubuffet harkens back to the tradition of garden follies.

Left: This work by Zhang Huan playfully commands the landscape.

Above: Joel Shapiro's angular figure contrasts joyfully with the vertical columns of the surrounding trees.

Scaffold Figure by Kiki Smith emerges from the shrubs at a woodland edge.

Formal structure and contrasting textures are juxtaposed at the entrance to the Gould garden.

GOULD GARDEN

GREENWICH, CONNECTICUT

Greenwich is a place associated in the popular imagination with grand houses and vast manicured lawns. What Jamie and Dale Gould started with twenty years ago, however, was a venerable, but tiny, early nineteenth-century saltbox teetering atop a steep, west-facing ridge. Below lay seven and one-half acres of field and woodland and the remains of an old chicken farm. The challenge was to integrate the house and landscape, to tame the slope without entirely domesticating it.

The Goulds hired Oscar Sandoval of Stamford, Connecticut, to terrace the slope with a series of stone and masonry retaining walls and steps. Although some of the stones incorporated were massive, clean lines and careful finish thwarted any impression of heaviness. The resulting terraces, as they stepped down from the house, provided opportunities for a vegetable and cutting garden, a swimming pool, and a perennial border, as well as giving access to the field below and to the west of the house.

Landscape architect James Doyle contributed a plan for the property, but the underlying theme was very much an expression of the owners' tastes. Jamie Gould, a co-owner of the renowned firm of Rogers and Goffigon, manufacturer of all-natural luxury textiles, wanted something as subtly textured as one of his own creations. What he did not want was a garden that was either entirely structured and formal, or one that was entirely wild. Nor did he want a compromise. Instead he and his wife juxtaposed elements of each, energizing the garden with the resulting tension of opposites.

A terrace immediately below the house, for example, had been planted with an allée of meticulously trimmed conical yew trees. The result reminded Jamie of a Christmas tree farm, until he recalled a garden he had visited in Paris, where such topiaries had been set amid a field of wildflowers. So the Goulds replaced the

91

turf that surrounded the yews with a tousled rectangle of meadow. Structured, yet wild.

Similarly, when a collection of heirloom apple trees was installed in the field below the ridge, the Goulds surrounded them with meadow. Garden designer Deborah Nevins infiltrated the grasses with spring flowering bulbs—fritillaries and early blooming narcissi, as well as species of roses such as the primrose-yellow–flowered *Rosa primula* and the pink-blossomed *Rosa moyesii* for a late spring, early summertime show. The result was a similar tension between the formality of the carefully pruned trees and the romantic spontaneity of the surrounding meadow.

Nevins also helped the Goulds with planting the forecourt in front of the house, separating it from the road with a file of Japanese hornbeams (*Carpinus japonica*), small, graceful trees that in springtime bear pendulous, lantern-like green fruits. And she reorganized and replanted the perennial border. There, amid a frame of sculpted boxwoods, she installed a collection of uncommon plants such as yellow wax bells (*Kirengeshoma palmata*), a pale yellow–flowered summer bloomer from Korea, and plume poppy (*Macleaya cordata*), another east Asian perennial, a stately eight-footer that bears airy panicles of creamy flowers in late summer. Structure was supplied not only by the boxwoods and a surround of clipped hedges, but also by stone paving interplanted with thyme. Inside was "a wilder look," according to Nevins, "Very abundant and beautiful colors. Not bright colors; there are no yellows and oranges. It's mainly blue, white, and pink."

When the Goulds downsized, putting the property on the market in 2018, the garden proved a major selling point with the new owners, who have not only maintained what was there, but even retained the same stone mason. Thus, this garden lives on.

Meadow grasses interwoven with wildflowers soften the formality of an allée of conical yews, lending an air of romantic spontaneity to this garden terrace.

Left: Counterpoised hedges endow
the entrance to the perennial border
with a monumental elegance.

Above: Within the perennial border,
designer Deborah Nevins introduced
a wilder look.

Above: Meadow grasses flank the
path to the swimming pool.

Right: Boxwood spheres punctuate
the perennial border.

Above: Stone steps lead to the
apple orchard.

Right: A flowery meadow envelops
the orchard's heirloom apple trees.

Left: Stone walls and steps define and unite the different areas of this steeply sloping site.

Above: Potted flowers soften the line of a stone wall.

Yellow flag iris and other water-loving plants adorn a small pond. Stone walls follow the contours of the basin, terminating with an arched stone bridge.

HAWKS NEST

CHAPPAQUA, NEW YORK

There wasn't much there other than the bones of the natural landscape when, in 1992, Larry Lederman and Kitty Hawks purchased the four-acre property that would become the Hawks Nest. There was a lot of lawn, studded with notable mature trees—maple, oak, tulip, and pine—plus a woods with stone outcrops and a stream tumbling down through a gorge to a small reservoir. Rather than commissioning a plan, Hawks and Lederman decided to live with and observe the land to let it inform the next steps.

This is not so different from what Hawks does in her acclaimed interior design practice. She seeks not to stamp a client's residence with a signature style, nor does she make it homogeneous. One room follows comfortably from the last, but each is distinct. She wants to make the whole look like it evolved over time.

Certainly, she followed an evolutionary style in the development of this garden. The irregular and sloping topography did not lend itself to a formal scheme. Instead, the swells and dips of the land created distinct areas, each of which has been treated differently, largely in response to available sunlight. Paths were put down according to those traversed instinctively by the couple and their dogs.

The evolutionary process also applied to the extent of the site. When they acquired an additional six acres of wetland on one side of the original property and later two more acres on the other side, the landscaping possibilities became apparent.

On the wetland Lederman first recognized the opportunities of the stream bed by having a small pond dredged and spanned by an arched stone bridge, and then by adding a series of falls leading through the gorge and finally to the reservoir. The last parcel was a flat sunny piece on which they placed a small greenhouse and a rose garden.

There are chairs throughout the garden where its owners sit and consider the landscape. The principal vista, a view of the reservoir from the house, was enriched early on by lacing the top of the reservoir's dam with a Miscanthus grass. In late summer the grass bears an exquisite cloud of airy pink seed heads, but in spring is quite unsightly. Hawks complemented it by planting forsythia, which blazes sun yellow in March and is magical when there is an early spring snow. A garage set into a berm near the front of the house was made the subject of a disappearing act: a layer of soil was laid across its roof and planted so that it appeared just a slight swell in the land.

Shaded areas beneath the trees where the grass grew poorly were replanted with groundcovers—nothing too exotic, just pachysandra, astilbe, and hosta—so that these islands of greenery lend a richness to the property as they grow and change shape following the canopies of the overhanging trees.

As the garden evolved, so too did Hawks's feel for the landscape. Indeed, at the beginning of the process she was relatively inexperienced, though she would draw on summers spent in England and a sojourn in California. She educated herself with catalogs and books, first mostly looking at images, but then returning to read the texts as she became more immersed in the gardening process. Books on English, French, and Italian gardens as well as on the work of notable designers such as Vita Sackville-West, Piet Oudolf, and Tom Stuart-Smith have informed the Hawks Nest. It is, as are all gardens, a work in progress awaiting more learning and more growth.

View of the reservoir from the house; the dam is topped with Miscanthus grass, which bears airy pink flowerheads in late summer and fall.

Left: Paralleling the Miscanthus grass is a hedge of forsythia that bursts into brilliant yellow bloom in early spring.

Above: The dam through the trees.

Left: Climbing hydrangea by the entrance court in spring.

Right: The entrance court overlooking a woodland gorge.

Left: Chairs provide vantage points from which to consider the garden.

Right: Notable trees give the garden an air of maturity.

Left: The rose garden boasts a collection of David Austin roses: 'Graham Thomas,' 'Jude the Obscure,' 'Cardine Mill,' 'Golden Celebration,' and 'Lady Emma Hamilton.'

Above: Winter reveals the structure of the rose garden.

Above: A sitting area outside the greenhouse centers on a crabapple whose colorful fruits persist through the winter; the red hedge is burning bush.

Right Blue star in its yellow fall foliage lines the walkway to a guest house.

Stones collected in the surrounding woods anchor this point overlooking the lake.

INNISFREE

MILLBROOK, NEW YORK

It's a garden born of an epiphany. Walter and Marion Beck had been searching for years for a model from which to draw the landscape of Innisfree, their retreat on a nine hundred–acre tract in Millbrook, New York. They had considered creating Anglo-inspired gardens to match the English-style manor house they had built, but they rejected that idea as too obvious. Then, on a trip to London in the early 1930s, Walter Beck encountered in the British Museum scrolls depicting the garden of eighth-century poet, painter, and musician Wang Wei.

Arranged around meandering interconnected paths, Wang Wei's garden was a complex of discrete, inward-looking features that Beck described as "cup gardens." The experience of navigating them was to be an *Alice in Wonderland*–style wander through magical episodes, according to Lester Collins, the young landscape architect whom the Becks commissioned to realize their plan. Each area was separate yet linked, often by common elements such as the native stone, or by the paths and bridges.

Collins, who had spent two years touring Asian gardens before studying landscape architecture at Harvard, was one of a very few American landscape professionals of the time versed in Chinese gardens. Yet what he and the Becks created in Millbrook was not explicitly Chinese. Instead, they used stones collected on the estate as well as trees, shrubs, and perennials to fashion a series of tableaux along the shore of a forty-acre glacial lake.

True greatness, however, came to Innisfree only after the death of the Becks, Walter Beck in 1954 and Marion Beck in 1959. They had hoped to leave the house and grounds as a place for the study of "the garden arts," but instead left behind some $200,000 in debt. Collins managed to raise money to discharge the debts and opened the garden to the public. He pulled down the house and eliminated the most extravagant of the Becks' fancies, such as the moss garden, which had required the attention of two gardeners.

These strictures, however, led Collins to an inspired design that was decades ahead of its time. He continued the cup garden motif, but made his additions more in harmony with the natural ecology of the site. He worked with the stone, contrasting built elements with the native outcrops, and, notably, he also worked with natural habitats, removing the overhanging trees from a wetland to enable the land to express itself as a rich "bog garden." Similarly, in Marion Beck's prized rock garden, he allowed a Darwinian competition that resulted in a self-sustaining tapestry of adapted plants. To keep the lake water free from algal blooms, Collins began pumping it uphill to a reservoir that the Becks had built and then let gravity pull it downhill through fountains and wetlands to be filtered naturally, the nutrients in it feeding the gardens. The effects are simple but ingenious: the fountains that recycle the filtered lake water also create pockets of humidity relished by primulas and ferns that formed carpets within the landscape. This was long before ecological gardening became a recognized discipline.

Collins's style of planting was modernist, but without the hard, artificial forms that characterize so many gardens of that school. Notable in this respect is a small grove of Bradford pears that are clipped annually so that the shadows they cast are a pattern of disks that rearrange themselves as the sun moves across the sky.

Collins supervised the garden until his death in 1993. Afterward, Innisfree remained under the care of first his wife and then his son until 2018. Today, the gardens, encompassing some 185 acres, are under the management of the Innisfree Foundation, whose goal is to preserve and continue the Collinses' work.

Collins's modernist planting includes this small grove of Bradford pears, clipped to cast a pattern of disk-shaped shadows that re-arrange themselves as the sun moves across the sky.

Left: By removing overhanging trees, Collins transformed a wooded wetland into this bog garden.

Right: A fall view down to the lake.

Above: A great oak shades a summertime retreat.

Right: A gravel road separates a rocky upland and a low-lying wet meadow.

Left: A mop-headed black willow punctuates and anchors this "cup garden."

Above: The same willow is as a reference point to relate an upper cup garden to the lower.

Above: Imaginative stonework such as this "circular grotto" enhances Innisfree's landscape.

Right: A cluster of paper birch trunks furnishes a pastoral focal point.

Iroki's maple collection includes more than 1,000 distinct types of these beautiful trees, out of an estimated worldwide total of 1,400.

IROKI

MOUNT KISCO, NEW YORK

It is the only physical possession in his life, says Michael Steinhardt, that gives him pleasure. Indeed, as he speaks of the garden he and his wife, Judy, share, the image of an Eden-like landscape, one filled with seasonal beauty and fruitfulness, emerges. There is every color and type of berry that is hardy in its climate, from blueberries to *fraises des bois*, a three hundred–tree orchard filled with vintage apples, pears, peaches, nectarines, and cherries, and a lotus garden where these sacred flowers are induced to flourish and bloom. And the feature for which this garden is famed in horticultural circles, one of the most comprehensive collections of Japanese maples anywhere.

Michael Steinhardt grew up in the concrete cityscape of Brooklyn, and it was only as an adult that he came to gardening, but his passion has grown steadily since he purchased sixteen acres in northern Westchester County in 1978. Three times Steinhardt has added adjacent properties, so that today the garden comprises fully fifty-eight acres. The name came with the acquisition of the third parcel, which had been the home of novelist Theodore Dreiser and which he had called Iroki. Dreiser's stone house survives only as ruins, ornamented now with plantings of tulips and wisteria, but his writing studio, a small cabin, remains intact.

If it included only the Japanese maple collection, this still would be a remarkable garden. Occupying approximately nine acres, this collection includes more than 1,000 distinct types of these beautiful trees, out of an estimated worldwide total of 1,400. Steinhardt seeks the best specimen of each, something unique, and makes regular shopping trips to the premier nurseries in the Pacific Northwest. He and his staff have also kept an eye out for specimens nearer to home, most recently sending a team to dig and transplant two hundred-year-old specimens of cutleaf Japanese maples (*Acer palmatum* var. *dissectum*) from a residential lot that was being redeveloped in Scarsdale, New

York. The maple grove is beautiful in every season, from budbreak in spring to the flaming foliage colors in autumn and the twisted branch and trunk forms revealed in winter.

However impressive, this is only a beginning. Other enthusiasms include a notable conifer garden with collections of pines (*Pinus*), firs (*Abies*), Japanese false cypresses (*Chamaecyparis*), and umbrella pines (*Sciadopitys verticillata*); an alpine garden; an extensive woodland garden filled with spring ephemerals such as trilliums and hardy orchids, and afterward peonies, hostas, and ferns; a yellow garden with plants of yellow-variegated foliage, flowers, and berries; and a collection of fall-blooming hardy camellias. Exotic animals—antelope, camels, ostriches, and zebras—roam the grounds, and an extensive aviary houses a host of fowl such as Egyptian ibis and Siberian cranes. A brook, crossed by a Chinese bridge, runs down from pool to pool, through a pond inhabited by enormous koi, and finally into a lake that serves as a home for black swans.

Set up on a hill is a *Big Bambu* sculpture that Judy and Michael commissioned from twins Mike and Doug Starn; this is an enormous structure of bamboo poles featuring a ramp for access to the top with seating areas along the way to a view platform at the summit.. Surprises of this sort are a favorite feature for the owners. Equally, Steinhardt appreciates what he calls "memorable moments." These include effects such as the whole hillside of *Hosta plantaginea* with its broad, glossy leaves and fragrant white blossoms, and the huge swaths of azure monkshood (*Aconitum carmichaelii* 'Arendsii'), whose rich purple flowers appear at the same time that the Japanese maples color in the fall. Certainly, Iroki is a landscape of countless moments no gardener could forget.

This huge pine sets the curve of the road, which leads, at right, to the conifer collection and, at left, to the Japanese maple collection; beyond is the apple orchard in full bloom.

Left: Swamp rose mallow overlooks a pond which, is home to a flock of black swans.

Above: A section of the conifer collection.

133

Above: Water spills off the edge of
a cantilevered stone.

Right: Steppingstones cross the pond
amid shade and the sound of running
water.

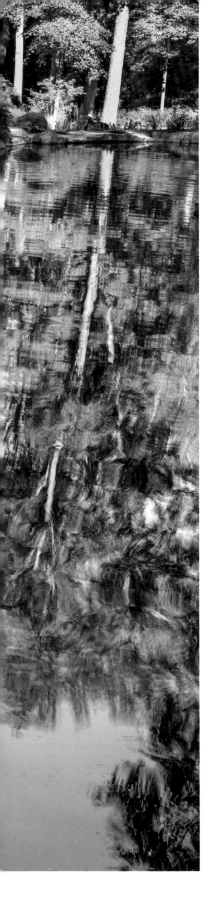

Left: Flashes of gold and white enliven a woodland koi pond.

Right: Mike and Doug Starn's *Big Bambu* offers a stepped climb to a viewing platform.

A path through the Japanese maple collection in spring.

The extraordinary collection of maples fills its woodland with a blaze of innumerable shades of reds, oranges, and golds in fall.

An arched, vermilion bridge is a graceful nod to their Japanese heritage.

Left: View from the maple collection to an enclosure in the Steinhart zoo, where zebras and camels graze.

Above: Writer Theodore Dreiser's writing studio.

A garden pavilion in the *Sukiya* style of sixteenth-century Japan. This simple and rustic architectural style was prized by Japanese nobility.

JAPANESE GARDEN AT KYKUIT

POCANTICO HILLS, NEW YORK

It is a world apart. Leaving behind the stately, Beaux-Arts landscape of the Rockefellers' Kykuit estate, visitors pick their way down a series of rustic stone steps, thread a narrow gap in an evergreen hedge, and find themselves in a Japan of long ago. Gnarled yet still graceful maples nod over a stream that tumbles through mossy rocks. A traditional pavilion overlooks a pool. Carefully chosen rocks emerge from raked white gravel in a Zen-inspired contemplation garden. To visit the Japanese garden at Kykuit is truly a transporting experience.

The garden's origins lie in a fashion set by the international expositions of late nineteenth- and early twentieth-century America. The young nation was looking outward, and in the process its public became fascinated with the cultures of Asia, in particular Japan. Japanese villages, temples, and gardens were a feature of these public spectacles, from the 1876 Centennial Exposition in Philadelphia to the 1904 Louisiana Purchase Exposition in St. Louis. Infected by this enthusiasm, owners of private estates began to include "Japanese" gardens in their landscapes. John D. Rockefeller Jr., who was embellishing the family's estate overlooking the Hudson River was not immune to fashion, and in 1908, he and his architect, William Welles Bosworth, installed a garden in the Japanese tradition of "hill-and-pond" gardens to the west of the main house. Seeking out the best advice, Rockefeller employed a Japanese craftsman to build the tea house and hired a Japanese gardener to realize the details of the landscape.

A thorough and insightful makeover came in the 1960s when John D. Rockefeller Jr.'s son Nelson and his sister-in-law Blanchette took the garden in hand. Blanchette Rockefeller in particular had a deeper understanding of Japanese culture, cultivated during annual visits to Japan and a extended stay in 1955. Together, she and Nelson Rockefeller moved the original tea house to another area of the estate and commissioned architect Junzō Yoshimura to construct a replacement, a compact garden pavilion in the *sukiya* style of sixteenth-century Japan.

They also hired David Harris Engel, an American who had studied in Kyoto with Tansai Sano, a garden master whose family had tended the famous dry garden at Ryōan-ji for six generations. Engel reorganized and refurbished the garden, transforming it into a two-acre "stroll" garden that invites visitors to follow paths through a succession of calculated experiences and sensations.

Different pavements—Japanese tiles set on end, fieldstone, and even worn cobblestones rescued from a street renovation in Albany, New York—change the stride and sensation of walkers as they progress through the garden. The spaces expand and contract as you cross and recross the stream and wind round the pools, and the planting and stonework have been arranged to ensure that nothing is completely revealed at any one vantage point, fostering a sense of mystery. A keynote of this garden is its sensuality: the textures of the weathered stones and mosses, the sound of the falling water, the rustle of bamboos in the wind, and the profile of a maple leaf floating in a pool.

Unlike many western gardens, the goal of this garden is not to reproduce or tame nature. Rather, as Engel explained in a 2013 essay, it "becomes a series of abstractions . . . a distillation of the vast world outside, yet subtly revealing the hand of man." This balance makes a visit to Kykuit's Japanese garden a powerful and spiritual experience.

An ancient maple lends a venerable air to a stream and a stone bridge.

Left: Sheared azaleas line the path
to the garden pavilion.

Above: The limbs of a Japanese maple
frame a view of the dry garden.

149

Right: The dry garden.

Above: Stones set in gravel form the
path that skirts the dry garden.

Left: Rustic stone steps climb through the clipped shrubs.

Right: A line of steppingstones edges the stream, occasionally crossing through the water.

Left: This broad path welcomes visitors to the garden.

Above: Boulders flanking the stream control the view from the stepping-stones so that each turn brings a surprise.

Overleaf: A surviving maple from the original planting of the garden.

A view of the lake from the house.

MERRIN GARDEN

CORTLANDT MANOR, NEW YORK

Change is the constant in this lakeside landscape. "If you feel a garden is completed," observes the owner, "then it's going to be on the downgrade from then on."

This garden was born more than thirty years ago, when Edward and Vivian Merrin purchased the property as a family retreat, a place where children and then grandchildren could join the couple for swimming and relaxing. Edward Merrin had well-developed aesthetic sensibilities: a dealer in pre-Columbian art and antiquities, he was renowned in his profession for his eye. He had never gardened, however. Indeed, he had never felt the need until the "wonderful" large trees on his new property inspired him.

At the suggestion of a client, Merrin invited with the then-young landscape architect, Patrick Chassé for a visit. His reaction, as Merrin recalls, was "I like the property very much. If you want to do a great garden, I'll work with you. If you don't want a great garden, I'm not your man."

Merrin opted for greatness, and there began a collaboration that continues to this day. Chassé worked closely with Merrin for the first five years, and still comes for consultations a couple of times a year. Chassé organized the landscape and contributed features such as a glass-enclosed overlook behind the house that provides a breathtaking bird's-eye view out over the lake. A formal pool was installed to host a planting of dozens of lotuses, which bear spectacular flowers that, as Merrin notes, have been worshipped for four thousand years. In the spring of 2019, a circular enclosure was installed in this, a pool within a pool, where the water is heated to foster the growth of the world's largest species of water lily, *Victoria amazonica*. As its name suggests, this plant hails from the Amazon basin; in Merrin's warmed water, the leaves grow like huge green platters to a width of three and one-half feet.

Around the house are arranged homages to various favorite plants: a tree peony garden, a display of carnivorous plants, and a succulent garden that is installed every spring, and then disassembled in the fall so that the frost-sensitive plants can overwinter under cover. This succulent garden changes every year, as new plants catch Merrin's eye and become a part of the display.

New developments also include the renovation of an orchard that yields fifteen types of apples and ten types of Asian pears, and a formal cutting garden that has joined the existing vegetable garden. Permanent fixtures lend stability: a pergola, a compact bamboo grove, woods filled with mountain laurels and rhododendrons, and lakeside plantings designed to stabilize the bank. Sometimes Merrin is opportunistic. When a hurricane felled trees, he pulled and assembled the stumps in a sculptural display around a bench.

The garden changes seasonally: the long, linear entranceway, for example, catches fire in spring with flowering shrubs and spring bulbs, while the lotus pond is more the focus in high summer.

Merrin's background as a collector of beautiful objects has an obvious relevance to this garden. Yet he had a lot to learn. When he began, he says, he didn't understand space. "A piece of sculpture is finite," he explains. "A painting has four sides." However, "a landscape is unending. You have to look at it in a completely different way." That takes someone with a sense of "grandeur and size."

That is what he has gathered from working with Patrick Chassé and from experimenting on the ground with his garden. Renowned in his business as the man with the best eye, Merrin has learned to look a different way in his woodland retreat.

Dogwoods bloom as the willows show first leaves on the path to the pavilion.

Left: Deciduous azaleas in bloom along the path from the road to the house.

Above: A bench offers a woodland respite amid azaleas and rhododendrons.

Left: Rhododendrons flank a path to the lake; lower limbs were removed from the trees to emphasize their exuberant forms

Right: A cluster of river birches marks a bend in the path from the pavilion to the house.

164

Left: Tucked into the trees, the house rests unobtrusively on the site. Below is the greenhouse.

Above: A curved stairway provides easy access from the house to the lake.

Sacred lotuses blend with tropical
water lilies in the pool adjacent
to the house; a Japanese-inspired
boardwalk invites a stroll among
the lotuses.

Left: A curved glass wall encloses this overlook.

Above: Vivian Merrin planted this island in the lake.

171

A crabapple shelters a path down into the garden at River Hills.

RIVER HILLS

BEDFORD, NEW YORK

Fifteen years ago, Leslie Needham took herself for a client. Trained as a landscape designer at the New York Botanical Garden, Needham had been busy creating gardens for others but now turned to her own property. She and her husband, John, had been living in River Hills, their three hundred-year-old house in Bedford, for a couple of years, time that Needham had spent becoming intimate with the farmhouse and its site overlooking the Mianus River Gorge.

Like many houses of its era, River Hills was inward looking and not well connected to the landscape. Correcting this became a primary goal, but Needham wanted to do so without detracting from the main view, eastward from the house toward the gorge. Fortunately, working for herself, creating a master plan that would restrict her to a set approach was not necessary. Instead, she could take her time and let the garden develop organically, unfolding in tandem with the house.

She and her husband transformed a glassed-in living room on the east side of the house into a porch to highlight the gorge view. They fenced the property to exclude deer, but used a sufficiently coarse mesh that the foxes, rabbits, and turtles could pass through and stop by. Indeed, the wildlife population grew steadily, for another of Needham's projects was to replace the lawn with plants more hospitable to pollinators and the insects that attract and support a rich and diverse bird population.

Another early project was to replace a rough path down the east-facing slope with stone steps framed with finials to create an invitation to a small orchard of three apple trees below. The orchard she reinforced with plantings of fourteen more trees: apples, peaches, plums, pears, and a mulberry and native pawpaw. She terraced the slope, and planted part as a dry garden of perennials and elsewhere with ornamental edibles and annuals—lettuces, figs, herbs, annual flowers, and dahlias. Because the slope faces away from the house, this does not distract from the view of the gorge, but when seen from below, it creates a stepped pedestal of flowers and foliage on which the house seems to rest. This hidden planting area also affords Needham a place in which to indulge her playful side, as she changes the planting from year to year.

Needham has enjoyed filling the garden with different experiences. When, for example, her husband established an office with French doors leading out to the north side of the house, Needham tore up the adjacent turf, installing an outdoor dining area sheltered by pleached plane trees, replanting the area beyond with native grasses and informally disposed, pollinator-friendly perennials to create a soft, low meadow.

Perhaps the most notable feature of this garden is the wealth of bloom from spring to fall. The display begins with redbuds (including a white *Cercis canadensis* 'Alba'), magnolias (the fragrant, yellow-flowered magnolia 'Elizabeth' that Needham and her husband planted more than a dozen years ago has done especially well), and dogwoods and viburnums, which give way to the blossoming of the fruit trees in the orchard. Hydrangeas—oakleaf, 'Annabelle', 'Limelight', and 'Tardiva'—furnish flowers throughout the summer and the fall, and Needham had layered in hearty perennials suitable to the rustic setting such as alliums, Joe Pye weed, amsonia, woodland phlox, milkweeds, and asters, as well as ferns for foliage interest.

Throughout this transformation, Leslie Needham was careful to respect the integrity of the site. New stone walls were created with materials gathered on the property, the view was preserved intact, and outlying areas of the landscape she kept more natural, using meadows and woodland walks to transition from domesticated to the natural. This is a garden that, despite its richness, rests easily on the land.

Hydrangeas edge a path with summertime bloom.

Above: A dining terrace shaded by
pleached London plane trees adjoins
the north side of the house.

Right: Coneflowers and rose campion
blend in a colorful tangle of flowers
and foliage in the dry garden.

Left: Stone walls frame a vista of the Mianus River Gorge.

Above: The view across the orchard to the house.

Above: Wisteria graces the rear porch.

Right: Alliums and blue Siberian iris
cascade over a retaining wall at the
top of the orchard.

Above: A hornbeam hedge screening the swimming pool is a simple and effective visual transition to the woodland beyond.

Opposite: The same scene in very early spring highlights the beauty of the maple trees in bloom.

A Japanese maple backs this rich presentation of azaleas in flower.

ROCKY HILLS

MOUNT KISCO, NEW YORK

"You can control what is inside your house," Henriette Granville Suhr once observed to an audience at the New York School of Interior Design, "but you cannot control what is outside. It tells you what to do!"

Indeed, she was an expert on both inside and out. Born in Vienna in 1917, Henriette Suhr was raised and studied interior design in Paris before immigrating to New York in 1941. She worked at a series of department stores before beginning a long tenure at Bloomingdale's in 1949, where she managed the interior decorating department.

In 1956, she and her husband, William Suhr, conservator at the Frick Collection, purchased a thirteen-acre farm in Mount Kisco, New York, which they named Rocky Hills. Neither had gardened seriously before, but they applied their combined artistic talents to the organization and enrichment of the landscape around their new weekend house.

Although Suhr was practiced in imagining and creating rooms, she did not follow this familiar path in her gardening. Rather, she seemed to take her inspiration from the plants. She and William collected an outstanding and eclectic assortment of conifers, rhododendrons and azaleas, lilacs, tree peonies, irises, and others, as well as sixty or more distinct types of ferns, arranging them around existing mature specimens of black walnut and ash.

There is, not surprisingly in a garden cocreated by a conservator of old masters, a painterly use of color. Rocky Hills is tinted with a cool blue wash of forget-me-nots in spring, and a similarly lavish, if hotter, display of tawny daylilies in summer. The use of form, such as in the juxtaposition of the different dwarf blue conifers—prostrate, weeping, and upright—in another section, perhaps reflects Suhr's experience in balancing compositions in her decoration of rooms. The remarkable collection of magnolias, some of them quite rare, was certainly Suhr's doing; she rescued sixteen trees when the Brooklyn Botanic Garden closed its nearby Kitchawan research station in 1990, six years after her husband's death.

One of the garden's great assets is its age. After sixty-plus years of careful cultivation, many of the plantings have reached an impressive size. A compact grove of dawn redwoods that the Suhrs planted in the early years towers now, and even those plants which were purchased as dwarfs have proven that dwarf plants may be characterized by slow growth, but given sufficient time may reach a considerable size.

The style of the planting is personal and difficult to define. Informal certainly, but too elegant and ambitious to be classified as a cottage garden. Rules are broken: Suhr liked to dot tulips, usually reserved for formal beds, in living bouquets in meadow areas. Lilac standards, shrubs pruned to a single straight trunk with a round top, are also arranged in the midst of free-form plantings rather than confined, as they normally would be, to a geometrically laid out area of formality.

The Suhrs had left Manhattan to live at Rocky Hills full time in 1977, upon William's retirement from the Frick Collection. Although Henriette Suhr continued her professional consulting into the 1980s, by then the garden had become the center of their lives. In 1995 she began inviting the public into the garden as part of the Garden Conservancy's open days program. In 2009, she was honored by the Landscape Foundation with its Place Maker Award. In 2015, five months after her death, a conservation easement was transferred to the Westchester Land Trust, protecting Rocky Hills in perpetuity. The following year, Rocky Hills was sold to Barbara and Rick Romeo, who have lovingly maintained the garden and have continued the custom of opening it to the public one day a year in collaboration with the Garden Conservancy.

Tawny daylily blossoms run like a river through the garden.

Left: Forget-Me-Nots overlay the garden with a wash of blue in early spring.

Above: Deft placement of shrubs and dwarf trees balance the garden views, reflecting Henriette Suhre's experience as an interior designer.

Above: A stream brings abundant
moisture and lush growth to
the site.

Right: After sixty years, many of
the plantings, such as a weeping
Norway spruce and a mature dwarf
Alberta spruce, have reached an
impressive size.

Left: A platform set up for picnics overlooks the stream and a flowering quince.

Above: The planting at Rocky Hills is particularly rich in azaleas and rhododendrons.

Above: A rhododendron in bloom
by a gate.

Right: The grove of dawn redwoods
above a carpet of bluebells and
primroses.

A seeded meadow and woodland intersect next to a barn at AP Farm.

AP FARM

CROSS RIVER, NEW YORK

In 1993, when Adam Rose and Peter McQuillan purchased the fifty-eight acres in northern Westchester County that would become AP Farm, the land was neglected and unkempt, albeit supporting attractive patches of mature woodland. They immediately set to work to bring it to a fine state of fertility, hiring landscape architect Doug Reed of the firm Reed Hilderbrand to assist with laying out the grounds around the house they constructed. Rose and McQuillan have continued to get the best advice, taking counsel with noted native plantsman Rick Darke and bringing in Larry Weaner to create custom seed mixes for the ten-plus acres of meadows that they have planted. On-staff horticulturists Graham Glauber (the estate manager) and Jacqueline Lyons have further contributed to the design. The result is a landscape rich in calculated effects but still authentically rural.

In this setting, the perennial garden running eastward from the house strikes a frankly formal note. Long and linear, it is planted with repeated clusters of similar flowers to give it a rhythmic flow throughout the blooming season. Paralleling the perennial planting is a narrow rill that runs along until it cascades into a koi pond. Similarly linear is the file of linden trees (*Tilia tomentosa*) that borders the lawn to the south of the house.

To create topography and lend interest to an otherwise flat field, the soil excavated to make the cellar of the house was shaped into a knoll into which to insert a swimming pool. This knoll was planted with part of the suite of grasses that have proven so successful on this property, in this case prairie dropseed (*Sporobolus heterolepis*) and little bluestem (*Schizachyrium scoparium*) 'Standing Ovation'. These are particularly fine in late summer when the dropseed bears its open, branching panicles of coriander-scented flowers and the bluestem covers itself with a haze of purplish-bronze blossoms.

197

To the north of the house is "the north oval," an area densely planted with 250,000 plugs, mainly of grasses—the *Sporobolus* and the *Schizachyrium* as well as tufted hairgrass (*Deschampsia cespitosa*) 'Goldtau', a compact cultivar which has dark green leaves and airy golden flowers that bloom all summer, and a switchgrass (*Panicum*) 'Cape Breeze'. This last is also compact, with foliage that stays green well into fall while coloring reddish purple at the tips, and that bears puffs of tiny yellow-green flowers through the summer. Interplanted with these grasses are a variety of ferns and pockets of flowering perennials that enliven the feature and contribute vivid seasonal color.

Despite the lavish use of grasses, the greatest emphasis in this landscape has been on the trees. There's a fine collection of yellow- and white-flowered magnolias, a planting of yellowwoods (*Cladrastis kentukea*—notable for its pinnately compound foliage, panicles of fragrant white spring flowers, and yellow fall color) bordering a brick terrace at the front of the house, and the elegantly formal lindens marching off to the south. Other notable and choice woody plants flourishing on the farm range from Manchurian striped maple (*Acer tegmentosum*) to the dove tree (*Davidia involucrata*) of southwestern China, our native pawpaw (*Asimina triloba*), and silver bell (*Halesia diptera* var. *magniflora*). Nor have the natural woods been neglected. Careful pruning has removed dead limbs and given a healthy structure to the trees, while the terrain has been kept free of invasive plants and enriched with woodland perennials and ephemerals.

An exquisite effect is achieved where the grassland and the woods intersect, as in the meadow adjacent to a barn and the driveway from the road to the house. Bordered by a slow-moving stream shaded by planted willows and river birch, this area is austerely handsome in winter and lush in early spring. Here, the principle of creating calculated effects while emphasizing the land's intrinsic beauty shows to best advantage.

The mature woodland was groomed by pruning and enriched with plantings of perennials and ephemerals.

In spring, dogwood blossoms float
like butterflies in the woodland and
a border of tulips edges a patio.

Above: A knoll, created with earth excavated from the cellar of the house, is planted with viburnum.

Right: Behind the perennial garden a file of linden divide a broad lawn from a woodland strolling area.

The perennial garden runs east from the house. Repeated planting of identical flowers creates a strongly rhythmic pattern through the seasons.

Above: A broad lawn stretches
between a stone wall and the lindens.

Right: The knoll and its viburnums
in autumn.

Left: In the fall, tawny grasses and golden willows are punctuated by the red of maples.

Right: A beautifully crafted stone wall was inserted among the mature trees.

A formal path bordered by hornbeam leads to a steep stair up a beech- and oak-covered hillside.

SLEEPY CAT FARM

GREENWICH, CONNECTICUT

Twenty-six years have gone into Fred Landman's embellishment of Sleepy Cat Farm, and his garden is still growing and changing. Starting with six acres in 1994, Landman began to assemble a collection of features he admired on his travels, seeking the assistance of landscape architect Charles J. Stick to synthesize the many parts into a harmonious whole. The result is a cosmopolitan and eclectic landscape of classically inclined individual gardens that Landman has tucked into a beech- and oak-covered hillside so that a walk—and this is a landscape above all designed for walkers—becomes a series of delightful discoveries.

From its original area, Sleepy Cat Farm has gradually spread to thirteen acres as Landman has acquired adjoining properties. The heart, arguably, remains "the Golden Path," a looping promenade of tawny decomposed granite that takes the visitor past an Italianate grotto and a "celestial pavilion," then downhill past an array of Tibetan prayer wheels, a garden of ten thousand Japanese irises traversed by a zigzagging Japanese "spirit bridge," and ending at a hydrangea walk.

This remarkable journey, however, is just a beginning. Still to be enjoyed are the English-style perennial border, which is surrounded by decorative stone walls covered with hydrangea, climbing roses, *Clematis*, and boxwood, a Chinese pavilion that seems to float on a small island in a koi pond, and from there a walk between serpentine hedges of European hornbeam (*Carpinus betulifolia*) to a monumental statue of Atlas— what Landman calls "the East–West Path." And then still to come are a reflecting pool, a maze, and wisteria arbor, a half-timbered barn, a cascade, and a formal potager.

Behind all of this, to the south, is a recently acquired tract that Landman calls "the Back 40." There, an orchard of fruit trees set into a meadow supply the view for a limonaia, a linear masonry structure with a south-facing wall of glass, an Italianate greenhouse for

211

overwintering the lemon trees that Landman and horticulturist Alan Gorkin grow in tubs.

This is a complex of gardens to follow through the seasons. Wintertime, when the foliage has been stripped away, calls attention to the structure of the landscape, the linear beauty of the carefully inscribed hedges, arbors, and walks, the punctuation of the statuary. Springtime is brilliant; it brings a vivid display of color as more than four hundred thousand flowering bulbs produce wave after wave of bloom. The woodland is bejeweled then too with azaleas, sweet woodruff, toad lilies, silver bells, and witch hazel. In the Back 40, this season shades the meadow blue, with a thin line of white flowers and a smattering of red, an effect that Landman calls "painting with flowers."

Summer offers sensual details such as the fanning of a koi's fins as it rises to the surface of the pond, the bounty of the potager, the refreshing sound of falling water in the woodland stream, fountains, and the cascade. The colors of fall are those of foliages on the trees, native and exotic, that fill these thirteen acres, and the late-hanging fruits.

Time spent in this garden is meant to be leisurely: Landman has marked views and pausing points with more than a dozen benches and continues to add to this number.

"It's been a project of more than twenty-five years," Landman says of the garden. "A lot of effort has gone into it. One of my greatest joys is when other people come here and get to experience what I experience every day."

In winter, the structure of the gardens emerges: the serpentine hornbeams, the Chinese pavilion at right, and the Norman guest house to the rear.

Spring wreaths the garden with
lush plantings, including weeping
cherry boughs overhanging the
Chinese pavilion.

Above: An outdoor dining area at the guest house.

Right: The terrace overlooks the reflecting pool and the wisteria arbor beyond.

Left: Topiaries create a transition from the bold space of the reflecting pool to the intricacy of the labyrinth.

Above: Fred Landman calls the walk from the Chinese pavilion to a monumental statue of Atlas the "East–West Path."

Throughout the gardens, strong structure disciplines lush planting; here the early bloom of magnolias is framed by the serpentine hornbeam hedge.

AFTERWORD

A garden is a portal to the natural world, and, also and inevitably, a stand against nature's relentless encroachment. The gardens in this book stand out because they have been developed over many years and are mature and cherished. All are refuges and retreats to nourish the spirit. The commitment to them shows in their beauty, as does the pleasure they offer.

Each is close enough to my home to allow me to follow them in all seasons and light. In photographing them, my urge is to express my experiences of them. These are the most personal of the gardens that I have photographed. The owners often called on me to hurry over not to miss their wonderful moments. Such enthusiasm is stirring and infectious.

All the gardens are different. Some are simple in concept: plantings around water, an oasis. The sky and the lush plantings are reflected in the water and the reflections touched by the wind are ever changing. Thoughtfully done, the visual experience is complex and engaging. Others make dramatic gestures using formal structure, rooms with varied plantings or striking plant collections. Some rely on the landscape and objects strategically placed to enchant.

There are woodland gardens and gardens with extensive meadows. In the woodlands, sight lines are short, and flowering trees, colorful shrubs and plantings lead you from experience to experience.

In meadows. there is always a line of sight, and paths are mowed. The meadows are designed to be reflective of the changing light and responsive to the wind, as absorbing as looking at the many moods of water.

There are gardens whose mystery is in the plantings that do not announce themselves until the seasonal moment is ripe. It is like watching a wave build far at sea and roll toward you and then, and only then, do you realize power of the artful plantings and the unimagined variability that the seasons can deliver on a few well-designed and planted acres.

I am an observer, even in my own garden. My photographs make permanent records and at the same time try to uncover and express inherent sources of enchantment. What I know is that each day is different and no one day exposes all. Only over time do the gardens unfold in the seasons and does the light become revelatory. My inspiration is the belief that with patience, images can succinctly capture essence, plumb the ineffable, touch the well spring of wonder that birthed the gardens to begin with. That is what I seek each time and over time.

The photographs in this book are the light years, so to speak, of my experiences of these cherished gardens.

Larry Lederman